THE
TOTALLY
PANCAKES
& WAFFLES
COOKBOOK

THE
TOTALLY
PANCAKES
& WAFFLES
COOKBOOK

By Helene Siegel

CELESTIAL ARTS
BERKELEY, CALIFORNIA

The Totally Pancakes & Waffles Cookbook is produced by becker&mayer!, Ltd.

Printed in Singapore.

Cover design and illustration: Bob Greisen
Interior design and typesetting: Susan Hernday
Interior illustrations: Carolyn Vibbert

Library of Congress Cataloging-in-Publication Data:
Siegel, Helene.
     Totally Pancakes & Waffles / by Helene Siegel
     p.   cm.
     ISBN 0-89087-804-8
     1. Cookery (pancakes, waffles)   I. Title
     TX770.P34S53   1996
     641.8'15—dc20   96-33746
                                              CIP

Celestial Arts Publishing
P.O. Box 7123
Berkeley, CA 94707

Other cookbooks in this series:
The Totally Burgers Cookbook
The Totally Camping Cookbook
The Totally Chocolate Cookbook

CONTENTS

INTRODUCTION

My reluctance to prepare pancakes every day of the week can be traced to sheer self-interest. My problem is that the pancake maker inevitably ends up standing at the stove cooking while everyone else gets to sit down and gobble up the hottest, and therefore the best, pancakes. My other problem revolves around weight gain—something one should never think about when ingesting a good hot breakfast dripping with maple syrup and butter anyway.

Unfortunately, the alternatives are not so attractive either.

Frozen pancakes and waffles have so little character. The pancakes in restaurants as a rule are rubbery and oversized and require that you be fully dressed to eat them. And cold cereal, yogurt, and toast just don't cut it when the body cries out for something soothing and comforting first thing on a cold morning. Something that can pull the family together and send them steadfastly forward into the next week.

Like many American parents, I compromise. I do pancakes on weekends. I do them quickly and efficiently, and I heat the oven up to 200 degrees F to keep them all warm on a platter so we can eat them together. Occasionally, I even get my husband to make them.

This collection is chock-full of ideas to keep the griddle (and the waffle iron) humming along happily. There are sour rye pancakes for culinary sophisticates and chocolate chip and peanut butter versions for younger palates. There are vegetable, rice, and cheese pancakes for casual suppers and a giant, impressive, oven-baked apple pancake for dessert. There is even a pancake cake. All are easy to make, fun to eat, great to share, and really not too fattening. Just keep an eye on that maple syrup and butter!

ALL-AMERICAN
HOTCAKES

BASIC BUTTERMILK PANCAKES

Consider this an insurance policy—just in case you run out of mix. As for running out of buttermilk, add 1 tablespoon vinegar to a cup of low-fat milk for a substitute.

1 cup all-purpose flour
1 teaspoon baking soda
1 tablespoon sugar
$1/4$ teaspoon salt
$1^{1}/_{4}$ cups buttermilk
1 egg
2 tablespoons butter, melted
butter for coating

Combine flour, baking soda, sugar, and salt in mixing bowl. Mix with fork.

In another bowl, whisk together the buttermilk, egg, and melted butter. Add the flour mixture to liquid and stir just until combined.

Heat the skillet or griddle over medium-high heat. Lightly coat with butter. Drop batter,

¹/₄ cup at a time, on griddle, with plenty of space for spreading. Fry until bubbles form and break on the pancake's surface and the bottom is browned. Flip and cook just until done, about 1 minute more.

MAKES 12

VARIATIONS

For banana pancakes, cut a banana into ¹/₄-inch slices. Press 4 or 5 slices into pancakes a few seconds after pouring batter into pan. Flip to finish. Blueberries can be added in the same way or gently stirred into batter right before cooking

---

Pancake: A flat cake cooked on a greased griddle and browned on both sides.

> —*from* The Dictionary of American Food and Drink *by John Mariani*

CORNMEAL BLUEBERRY CAKES

*These substantial yellow cakes rise up high
and mighty.*

$1/2$ cup cornmeal
$1/2$ cup boiling water
1 egg
$1/2$ cup sour cream
$1/4$ cup milk
2 tablespoons vegetable oil
$3/4$ cup cake flour
2 tablespoons sugar
1 teaspoon baking powder
$1/4$ teaspoon baking soda
$1/4$ teaspoon salt
1 pint blueberries
oil for coating

Place the cornmeal in a small bowl. Pour in
the water and stir to evenly moisten.

In a large bowl, whisk together the egg, sour
cream, milk, and oil. Add the cornmeal and

whisk to combine.

In another bowl, combine the flour, sugar, baking powder and soda, and salt. Pour in the liquid ingredients and whisk to combine. Gently stir in the blueberries.

Heat the skillet or griddle over medium-high heat. Lightly coat with oil. Drop batter, $1/4$ cup at a time, on griddle, with plenty of space for spreading. Fry until bubbles form and break on the pancake's surface and the bottom is browned. Flip and cook just until done.

MAKES ABOUT 8

Let's be honest: unless you come from Rhode Island, a true Johnny Cake isn't worth making for anyone but yourself. They're tricky to make and no one will thank you for the effort—at least until they've acquired the taste.

—from Simple Cooking *by John Thorne*

CHOCOLATE CHIP PANCAKES

You may even be able to persuade children to skip the syrup when you serve these delicate chocolate goodies.

1 cup all-purpose flour
1 tablespoon sugar
1/4 teaspoon salt
1 teaspoon baking powder
1 cup milk
1 egg
1 teaspoon vanilla
1 tablespoon butter, melted
1/2 cup mini chocolate chips
confectioners' sugar for dusting
butter for coating

Combine the flour, sugar, salt, and baking powder in large mixing bowl.

In another bowl, whisk together milk, egg, vanilla, and butter. Add milk mixture to flour and gently whisk to combine. Gently whisk in chocolate chips.

Heat the skillet or griddle over medium-high heat. Lightly coat with butter. Drop batter, $1/4$ cup at a time, on griddle, with plenty of space for spreading. Fry until bubbles form and break on the pancake's surface and the bottom is browned. Flip and cook just until done, about 1 minute more. Dust with confectioners' sugar and serve.

MAKES 10

Basic Ingredients

For the recipes in this book, butter is always unsalted, eggs are extra large, and milk and buttermilk are low fat unless otherwise noted. Buttermilk and milk can be used interchangeably, but be sure to include baking soda (rather than powder) with the dry ingredients when using buttermilk.

DOUBLE WHEAT CAKES

These pancakes are quite light for a wheat cake. I like them with sliced bananas and good maple syrup.

$1/2$ cup whole wheat flour
$1/2$ cup all-purpose flour
2 teaspoons baking soda
2 tablespoons sugar
$1/4$ teaspoon cinnamon
$1/2$ teaspoon salt
1 tablespoon wheat germ
$1 1/4$ cups buttermilk
1 egg
1 tablespoon oil for coating

Combine flours, baking soda, sugar, cinnamon, salt, and wheat germ in large bowl. Mix with fork.

In another bowl, whisk together buttermilk, egg, and oil. Pour into flour mixture and gently whisk to combine.

Heat the skillet or griddle over medium-high heat. Lightly coat with oil. Drop batter, $1/4$ cup at a time, on griddle, with plenty of space for spreading. Fry until bubbles form and break on the pancake's surface and the bottom is browned. Flip and cook just until done, about 1 minute more.

MAKES 10

Better Batter

The key to light, tender pancakes is to barely mix the batter just to blend the ingredients. Like quick breads and muffins, pancakes do not call for strenuous beating. If necessary, most batters can sit on a counter or in the refrigerator for a few hours or even overnight. A thin batter can always be thickened with a tablespoonful or two of flour, and a thick batter can be thinned with milk.

SPICED OAT CAKES

Try these delightfully hearty, golden yellow pancakes with the homemade apricot sauce on page 87.

$3/4$ cup all-purpose flour
$1/2$ cup oat flour or finely ground oatmeal
1 tablespoon plus 1 teaspoon brown sugar
$1^1/2$ teaspoons baking powder
$1/2$ teaspoon salt
$1/4$ teaspoon cinnamon
$1/8$ teaspoon ground nutmeg
1 cup milk
1 egg
2 tablespoons butter, melted

Combine flour, oat flour, brown sugar, baking powder, salt, cinnamon, and nutmeg in large bowl.

In another bowl, whisk together milk, egg, and butter. Pour into flour mixture and whisk to combine.

Heat the skillet or griddle over medium-high heat. Lightly coat with butter. Drop batter, $\frac{1}{4}$ cup at a time, on griddle, with plenty of space for spreading. Fry until bubbles form and break on the pancake's surface and the bottom is browned. Flip and cook just until done, about 1 minute more.

MAKES 10

Griddle Savvy

When frying and turning pancakes, coat a hot pan or griddle with a fine film of oil or butter. Sprinkle a few drops of batter or water on the pan to test. (The water should bead up and the batter should fry immediately.) Always consider the first pancake the test case. Use it to adjust the temperature and gauge the batter. If it blackens, turn down the heat, and if it takes more than 2 minutes to cook, turn it up.

SOUR CREAM SILVER DOLLARS

These mild, light miniatures cook up just thick enough to hold a shape. Try serving with a dollop of fruit preserves.

2 eggs
1 cup sour cream
2 tablespoons sugar
$^1/_2$ cup all-purpose flour
$^1/_2$ teaspoon salt
$^1/_2$ teaspoon baking soda
butter for coating
confectioners' sugar for dusting

Combine all of the ingredients except butter and confectioners' sugar in a blender. Blend until smooth.

Heat the skillet or griddle over medium-high heat. Lightly coat with butter. Drop batter, 2 tablespoonfuls at a time, on griddle, with plenty of space for spreading. Fry until bubbles form and break on the pancake's surface and the bottom is browned. Flip and cook just until done, about 1 minute more. Dust with confectioners' sugar.

MAKES 16

Practice Makes Perfect
Turning pancakes just takes practice. Forget the fancy footwork; just keep your spatula close to the pan's surface and turn the cakes with a swift flick of the wrist.

LIGHTER THAN AIR LEMON CAKES

Save these lacy yellow pancakes for a special brunch and serve with "Raspberry Sauce" (see page 89) or a fine-quality berry jam.

2 eggs, separated
1/2 cup plain yogurt
grated zest of 1 lemon
2 tablespoons lemon juice
2 tablespoons butter, melted
3 tablespoons sugar
1/2 cup cake flour
1/4 teaspoon baking soda
1/4 teaspoon salt
confectioners' sugar
butter for coating

In large mixing bowl, whisk together egg yolks, yogurt, lemon zest and juice, butter, and sugar. Sprinkle on remaining ingredients, except the whites and confectioners' sugar, and whisk to blend.

In a clean bowl, whisk the egg whites until soft peaks form. Gently fold into batter.

Heat the skillet or griddle over medium-high heat. Lightly coat with butter. Drop batter, 1/4 cup at a time, on griddle, with plenty of space for spreading. Fry until bubbles form and break on the pancake's surface and the bottom is browned. Flip and cook just until done, about 1 minute more. Dust with sugar.

MAKES 12

CAPPUCCINO CAKES

For those who never get enough morning coffee. Try these rich cakes with "Mocha Sauce" (see page 91).

2 teaspoons instant espresso powder
1 tablespoon hot water
1 egg
$^3/_4$ cup milk
1 teaspoon vanilla
2 tablespoons butter, melted
$^3/_4$ cup plus 2 tablespoons all-purpose flour
1 teaspoon baking powder
3 tablespoons sugar
$^1/_4$ teaspoon salt
confectioners' sugar and grated chocolate for
    sprinkling
butter for coating

Mix together the instant coffee and water to dissolve.

Whisk together egg, milk, vanilla, butter, and espresso mixture in mixing bowl.

In another bowl, combine flour, baking powder, sugar, and salt. Add to liquid mixture and whisk to combine.

Heat the skillet or griddle over medium-high heat. Lightly coat with butter. Drop batter, $1/4$ cup at a time, on griddle, with plenty of space for spreading. Fry until bubbles form and break on the pancake's surface and the bottom is browned. Flip and cook just until done, about 1 minute more. Dust with sugar and sprinkle with chocolate.

MAKES 12

ALMOST JOHNNYCAKES

Rhode Island johnnycakes are made entirely of corn-meal, so they are even thinner and more fragile than these. Maple syrup is the topping of choice.

1 cup cornmeal
1 1/4 cups buttermilk
1 teaspoon baking soda
1/2 teaspoon salt
2 tablespoons honey
1 tablespoon corn or vegetable oil
1/4 cup all-purpose flour
oil for coating

Place the cornmeal in a mixing bowl. Add the buttermilk, baking soda, salt, honey, and oil. Whisk to combine and let sit 10 minutes.

Sprinkle in the flour and stir just to combine. Heat the griddle over medium-high heat. Lightly coat with oil. Pour batter, 2 tablespoonfuls at a time, on griddle, with plenty of space for spreading. Fry until bubbles form and break on the pancake's surface and the bottom is browned. Flip and cook just until done, about 1 minute more.

MAKES 20 SMALL CAKES

BUCKWHEAT PANCAKES

Buckwheat flour, available in health food stores, is not really a grain; it is the ground seed of an herb. Its distinctive vegetable scent and flavor are balanced here with wheat and orange. Top with maple syrup and sliced bananas or chopped nuts.

$1/4$ cup whole wheat flour
$1/4$ cup buckwheat flour
$1/2$ cup all-purpose flour
1 teaspoon baking soda
1 teaspoon baking powder
$1/2$ teaspoon salt
3 tablespoons brown sugar
2 eggs
1 cup buttermilk
2 teaspoons grated orange zest
3 tablespoons butter, melted

Combine the flours, baking soda and powder, salt, and brown sugar in a large mixing bowl. Mix with fork.

In another bowl, whisk together eggs, buttermilk, and zest. Pour into flour mixture and stir to combine. Pour in butter and gently whisk.

Heat the skillet or griddle over medium-high heat. Lightly coat with butter. Drop batter, $\frac{1}{4}$ cup at a time, on griddle, with plenty of space for spreading. Fry until bubbles form and break on the pancake's surface and the bottom is nearly black—these take a bit longer to cook than most pancakes. Flip and cook just until done, about 2 minutes more.

Makes 12

SOUR RYE CAKES

Top these dark, full-bodied pancakes with sliced oranges and maple syrup, or try "Orange Maple Syrup" (see page 93).

$^1/_2$ cup rye flour
$^1/_2$ cup all-purpose flour
1 teaspoon salt
1 teaspoon baking soda
$1^1/_2$ cups buttermilk
1 tablespoon vegetable oil
1 egg
1 tablespoon molasses
1 tablespoon grated orange zest
butter for coating

Combine flours, salt, and baking soda in large bowl. Mix with a fork.

In another bowl, whisk together buttermilk, oil, egg, molasses, and orange zest. Pour liquid ingredients into flour mixture. Whisk just to combine.

Heat the skillet or griddle over medium-high heat. Lightly coat with butter. Drop batter, $\frac{1}{4}$ cup at a time, on griddle, with plenty of space for spreading. Fry until bubbles form and break on the pancake's surface and the bottom is browned. Flip and cook just until done, about 1 minute more.

MAKES 14

OAT AND ALMOND CAKES

With their pebbly texture and excellent flavor, these favorites are delicious served with natural fruit butters or just sprinkled with confectioners' sugar and sliced almonds.

$1/2$ cup oat flour or finely ground oatmeal
$1/4$ cup all-purpose flour
$1/4$ cup finely ground almonds
2 tablespoons sugar
$1/2$ teaspoon salt
pinch of nutmeg
1 teaspoon baking soda
$1 1/4$ cups buttermilk
1 egg
$1/2$ teaspoon almond extract
2 tablespoons butter, melted
butter for coating

Combine flours, almonds, sugar, salt, nutmeg, and baking soda in large bowl. Mix with fork.

In another bowl, whisk together buttermilk, egg, almond extract, and butter. Pour into flour mixture and gently stir just to combine.

Heat the skillet or griddle over medium heat. Lightly coat with butter. Drop batter, $^1/_1$ cup at a time, on griddle, with plenty of space for spreading. Fry until bubbles form and break on the pancake's surface and the bottom is browned   these take a bit longer to cook than most pancakes. Flip and cook just until done, about 2 minutes more.

MAKES 14

Griddling Equipment

The art of pancake making is comfortably low-tech. All it takes is a couple of mixing bowls, a whisk, spatula, and mixing spoon, a ladle for pouring the batter, and a good, heavy, cast-iron frying pan or griddle. If you find yourself in the business of making pancakes regularly, and your stovetop does not come with a griddle, you may want to invest in an electric griddle, as I did. They are nonstick and heat up evenly and instantly to the correct temperature for foolproof pancake turning.

Electric waffle irons come in various sizes and configurations—hearts, circles, and squares being the most popular. Any and all will work well with the recipes. Look for nonstick surfaces that can be cleaned just by wiping off with a damp sponge. These recipes were tested on a 7-inch round Toastmaster iron that produces a classic round waffle, easily broken into quarters for smaller servings.

SAVORY PANCAKES

POTATO LATKES

In the old days, grandmothers hand-grated potatoes by the pound for these traditional Jewish pancakes served at Hanukkah. I suggest the finest shredding blade of the food processor for equally wonderful but much quicker, lacier pancakes. Serve with applesauce and sour cream. Don't make too far in advance. Nothing compares to potato pancakes fresh from the frying pan.

4 large baking potatoes, peeled and finely shredded
1 medium onion, grated
2 eggs, beaten
3 tablespoons all-purpose flour
1 teaspoon salt
$1/2$ teaspoon pepper
corn or peanut oil for frying
applesauce and sour cream for garnish

In large bowl, combine potatoes, onion, eggs, flour, salt, and pepper. Mix well with a spoon. Heat oven to 200 degrees F.

Pour the oil to a depth of $1/4$ inch in one or two large skillets. Heat over medium-high heat and spread paper towels nearby. Using 2 spoons, drop the batter by large spoonfuls into hot oil, flattening with the back of a spoon, to form 3-inch circles. (The trick to great latke frying is to keep straining, or spooning off, excess liquid from potato mixture as it sits.) Fry until golden brown on one side, then flip and cook the second side until golden brown. Drain on towels. To keep warm, transfer to baking sheet, in single layer, and reserve in oven up to 2 hours. Serve hot with applesauce and sour cream.

MAKES 3 DOZEN

TWO SIDES BROWN NOODLE PANCAKE

This large, blackened noodle pancake is traditionally used as a platform for a saucy stir-fry dish. If making in advance, let noodles dry, cover with plastic, and reserve in the refrigerator for a day.

 ½ pound spaghettini
 4 tablespoons peanut oil
 salt and sesame oil

Cook the pasta in a large pot of salted water. Drain and rinse well with cold water, fluffing the strands to separate. Spread the noodles in an even layer on a platter. Set aside, uncovered, at room temperature, until dry, at least 2 hours.

To fry, heat 2 tablespoons of the peanut oil in a large, heavy skillet over high heat. Spread the noodles in the pan in an even layer. Fry until bottom is crisp and brown. Using a spatula and the palm of your hand to hold the top, flip the pancake. Drizzle the remaining peanut oil along the pan's edges and fry until the bottom is brown and crisp. Slide onto a serving platter and season with salt and sesame oil. Top with a saucy stir-fry dish.

MAKES 1, SERVES 4

COTTAGE CHEESE CUTIES

These rich-tasting miniatures are light, fluffy, and surprisingly low in fat. They taste like a blintz without the stuffing, and are perfect just dabbed with a little jam.

3 eggs, separated
1 cup low-fat small curd cottage cheese
1/3 cup all-purpose flour
1 teaspoon baking powder
1/4 teaspoon salt
2 tablespoons milk
butter for coating
confectioners' sugar for dusting

Combine the egg yolks, cottage cheese, flour, baking powder, salt, and milk in mixing bowl. Beat with electric mixer to blend.

In a clean, dry bowl, whisk the egg whites until soft peaks form. Gently fold into batter.

Heat a skillet or griddle over medium-high heat and lightly coat with butter. Drop the batter by generous tablespoonfuls, and fry until bubbles form on the top and the bottom is golden. Flip and fry the second side until golden brown. Dust with sugar and serve.

MAKES 18

By Any Other Name . . .

In America, simple, fried flat cakes made from batter eventually got the nickname hoecakes (since they could be cooked on the flat blade of a hoe), which evolved into flapjacks, slapjacks, griddle cakes, and hotcakes. Meanwhile, miners and loggers like the legendary Paul Bunyan ate them by the bucketful; the colorful term "flannel cakes" came from the shirts they wore. And, of course, in Rhode Island a simple corn cake will always be called a johnnycake. For the sake of clarity: "hotcake" or "griddle cake" or "flapjack" is just another way of saying "pancake."

WILD RICE PECAN PANCAKES

These quick cakes highlight the crunchy, nutty quality of wild rice superbly. I like them as a small vegetarian meal, topped with yogurt and a good, hot tomato salsa.

2 cups cooked wild rice, cooled
1/4 cup chopped pecans
3 tablespoons diced onion
2 eggs, beaten
2 tablespoons all-purpose flour
1/4 teaspoon salt
freshly ground pepper
3 or 4 dashes Tabasco
vegetable oil for frying
plain yogurt and salsa for garnish

In a large bowl, combine rice, pecans, onion, eggs, flour, salt, pepper, and Tabasco. Mix well.

Pour oil to ¼-inch depth in large skillet. Heat over medium-high heat. Using 2 large mixing spoons, drop the batter by large spoonfuls, forming 3-inch pancakes. (Do not crowd the pan, and be careful of splattering oil.) Fry until deep golden, about 2 minutes each side. Drain on paper towels. Serve hot with yogurt and salsa.

MAKES 6 LARGE PANCAKES

Note: To cook wild rice, bring salted water to a boil, using 3 times the quantity of dry rice. (For 2 cups of rice, use ½ cup of rice and 1½ cups of water.) Add rice, reduce to a simmer, cover and cook until tender, about 45 minutes. Drain excess water. Allow to cool.

ARBORIO RICE AND PARMESAN CAKES

Here is a quick take on fried risotto patties. If you have leftover risotto in the refrigerator, skip the first step.

2 cups water
1 cup arborio rice
pinch salt
2 tablespoons butter
3/4 cup grated Parmesan cheese
1/2 medium onion, diced
2 eggs, beaten
1 1/2 cups bread crumbs
olive oil for frying
lemon wedges for garnish

Bring the water to a boil, stir in the rice and a pinch of salt, and reduce to a simmer. Cover and cook 15 minutes. Stir in butter, cheese, and onion and replace the cover. Transfer to a bowl, cover with plastic, and chill.

To fry, wet hands and pat out small flat patties. Dip first in egg and then in bread crumbs to coat. Shake off excess. Pour the oil into a large skillet to a depth of $1/4$ inch. Heat over medium-high. Fry until golden brown on both sides, about 6 minutes total. Drain on paper towels. Serve hot with lemon wedges.

MAKES 12

NAVAJO CORN CAKES

Topped with good spicy salsa and some sliced avocado, these sturdy corn pancakes make a nice vegetarian main course.

1½ cups cornmeal
½ cup all-purpose flour
½ teaspoon baking powder
¼ teaspoon baking soda
¾ teaspoon salt
1 egg
1 cup milk
½ cup sour cream
1 tablespoon honey
1½ cups corn kernels
oil for frying
salsa and sliced avocado for garnish

Combine cornmeal, flour, baking powder and soda, and salt in large mixing bowl.

In another bowl, whisk together egg, milk, sour cream, and honey. Pour into dry mixture and stir to blend. Gently stir in corn.

Heat large heavy skillet over medium-high heat and pour in oil to ¼-inch depth. Drop batter, ¼ cup at a time, into pan and fry until well browned and crisp on both sides, about 5 minutes total. Drain on paper towels. Serve topped with salsa and sliced avocado.

MAKES 12, SERVES 4 TO 6

Pancakes in America

Native Americans were already eating pancakes when the Europeans arrived. Their cakes were made of the native grain, cornmeal, and corn cakes became known as "Indian cakes." The Dutch brought over their traditional pannekoeken *or buckwheat cakes, and the English brought the tradition of Pancake Tuesday— wherein the first Tuesday before Lent, or Shrove Tuesday, was celebrated with a feast of rich, buttered flat cakes.*

ZUCCHINI PANCAKES

Dark and crisp on the outside and creamy on the inside, these rich vegetable pancakes need no embellishment. Serve as a side dish with grilled meats or fish, or as a light vegetable supper.

4 large zucchini, trimmed, unpeeled
1 large baking potato, peeled
$^1/_2$ onion, peeled
1 egg, beaten
$^1/_4$ cup all-purpose flour
1 teaspoon salt
freshly ground pepper
vegetable oil for frying

Finely shred zucchini, potato, and onion (the food processor is fine for this). Transfer to a large bowl. Add the egg, flour, salt, and pepper and combine well.

Meanwhile, pour oil to depth of $^1/_4$ inch in one or two large skillets. Heat over medium-high. Pressing out excess liquid occasionally, drop by large spoonfuls in oil. Reduce heat to medium-low and fry until blackened in spots, about 4 minutes per side. Drain on paper towels.

MAKES 15

To Freeze

Both pancakes and waffles can be made in advance and frozen—witness the many varieties in your supermarket freezer. To freeze your delicious homemade products, first cool on baking racks to prevent sogginess. Pack pancakes singly in thin plastic sandwich bags and then place the bags in a zipper-lock freezer bag. Pack waffles, stacked, in 1-gallon zipper-lock bags.

To defrost, place pancakes in a single layer on baking sheets and bake in preheated 350 degrees F oven for 10 minutes, turning once. For waffles, thaw thicker ones at room temperature for 15 minutes and then toast on a low setting. Thin waffles can go directly from freezer to toaster.

Waffling Tips

When it comes to making waffles, crisper and browner is invariably better. Beaten egg whites and more melted butter in the batter add crispness—as does a good hot iron. Let it preheat for 15 minutes and then keep the lid closed until about a minute or so after the light goes out and steam stops escaping.

To cook, pour about $1/2$ cup of batter onto the center of the iron, wait a second or two, and then spread with the back of a spoon or ladle out to the edges. Don't panic about spillovers, but do line the work counter with paper towels for easier cleanup. The sides of the iron can be easily wiped clean when you are done.

ALL-STAR WAFFLES

MIMI'S PURLOINED EMPIRE-BUILDING RAISED WAFFLES

This make-in-advance, hold-in-the-refrigerator batter produces the lightest, crispest, most perfect plain waffles anyone could ask for. The recipe comes from a friend, cartoonist Mimi Pond, who doesn't recall where she found it.

2 1/2 cups milk, warmed
1 (1/4-ounce) package dry yeast
1 teaspoon sugar
1 stick butter, melted
1 teaspoon salt
2 cups all-purpose flour
2 eggs, beaten
1/4 teaspoon baking soda
maple syrup for garnish

In a large mixing bowl, stir together ½ cup of the milk, yeast, and sugar. Let stand until foamy, about 5 minutes.

Add butter, remaining milk, salt, and flour. Stir to blend. Cover with plastic and let stand, at room temperature, overnight, or until nearly doubled (Do not worry about lumps in the batter.)

Just before cooking, stir in eggs and soda—this is a thin, smooth batter. Heat the waffle iron and pour on ½ to ¾ cup batter. Bake until golden and crisp. Serve with maple syrup. (The batter keeps in the refrigerator about 3 days.)

MAKES 8

To waffle: To talk foolishly or without purpose; to idle away time with talking.

CARROT RAISIN WAFFLES

Morning food doesn't get much better than these full-flavored, moist waffles—one of my favorites. They are so good that you may not need syrup; just top with some plain yogurt and raisins.

1 cup milk
2 eggs
3 tablespoons butter, melted
$1/4$ cup raisins
$3/4$ cup all-purpose flour
$1/4$ cup sugar
$2^1/2$ teaspoons baking powder
$1/4$ teaspoon salt
$1/2$ teaspoon cinnamon
$1/4$ teaspoon ground nutmeg
$1/4$ cup finely chopped walnuts
$1/2$ cup finely shredded carrots
maple syrup *or* plain yogurt, raisins, and
    honey for garnish

Preheat the waffle iron. Whisk together milk, eggs, butter, and raisins and set aside 15 minutes to plump.

Combine flour, sugar, baking powder, salt, cinnamon, and nutmeg in large mixing bowl. Mix with a fork.

Pour milk mixture into flour and stir to combine. Gently stir in nuts and carrots.

Pour onto the waffle iron and follow the manufacturer's instructions. Serve with maple syrup or a dollop of yogurt, sprinkled with raisins and honey.

MAKES 4

ORANGE CHOCOLATE CHIP WAFFLES

My four-year-old's favorite. He prefers a major drizzle of maple syrup, but more sophisticated palates might like orange marmalade.

1 cup all-purpose flour
1 teaspoon baking powder
$^1/_2$ teaspoon baking soda
2 tablespoons to $^1/_4$ cup sugar
$^1/_4$ teaspoon salt
1 cup milk
2 egg yolks
1 tablespoon orange liqueur
4 tablespoons butter, melted
$^1/_3$ cup mini chocolate chips
2 egg whites, beaten to soft peaks
confectioners' sugar and orange marmalade
  or "Orange Maple Syrup" (see page 93) for
  garnish

Preheat the waffle iron.

Combine flour, baking powder and soda, sugar to taste, and salt. Mix with a fork.

In another bowl, whisk together milk, yolks, orange liqueur, and butter. Pour into flour mixture and stir to combine. Gently stir in chips. Fold in beaten whites until they just disappear.

Pour onto the waffle maker and follow the manufacturer's instructions. Serve dusted with confectioners' sugar and a dollop of orange marmalade or with Orange Maple Syrup.

MAKES 4.

CHEDDAR BACON WAFFLES

Remember the taste of bacon dipped in maple syrup from those good old days before cholesterol? These splendid waffles recapture that sweet and salty memory without going overboard.

6 strips bacon
1/4 cup whole wheat flour
3/4 cup all-purpose flour
2 teaspoons baking powder
2 teaspoons sugar
1 1/4 cups milk
1 egg
3 tablespoons butter, melted
1/2 cup grated cheddar cheese
maple syrup for garnish

Fry, drain, and crumble the bacon. Set aside.

Preheat the waffle iron.

Combine flours, baking powder, and sugar in large bowl. Mix with a fork.

In another bowl, whisk together milk, egg, and butter. Pour into flour mixture and stir to combine. Gently stir in the cheese and bacon—the batter will be thick.

Pour onto the waffle maker and follow the manufacturer's instructions.

MAKES 4

PUMPKIN SPICE WAFFLES

For pumpkin pie fans, here are all the familiar flavors baked into a deliciously crisp waffle—inspired by Sarabeth's Kitchen in New York City.

1/2 cup canned pumpkin purée
1/2 cup sour cream
1/2 cup milk
2 eggs, separated
1/2 stick butter, melted
2 tablespoons brown sugar
3/4 cups plus 2 tablespoons all-purpose flour
1 teaspoon baking powder
1/4 teaspoon baking soda
1/4 teaspoon salt
1/2 teaspoon cinnamon
1/4 teaspoon ground nutmeg
maple syrup *or* sour cream, honey, chopped pecans, and raisins for garnish

Preheat the waffle iron.

Whisk together pumpkin, sour cream, milk, egg yolks, butter, and brown sugar in large bowl.

In another bowl, combine the flour, baking powder and soda, salt, cinnamon, and nutmeg. Add the dry ingredients to the pumpkin mixture and stir to combine.

In a third bowl, whisk the egg whites until stiff peaks form. Gently fold the whites into the batter.

Pour onto the waffle maker and follow the manufacturer's instructions. Serve with maple syrup or the suggested garnishes.

MAKES 4

TOASTED ALMOND WAFFLES

For a special treat, serve these light waffles with
"Raspberry Sauce" (see page 89) or vanilla-scented
whipped cream instead of maple syrup.

1 cup plus 2 tablespoons all-purpose flour
$^1/_2$ cup finely ground almonds
1 tablespoon baking powder
1 tablespoon plus 2 teaspoons sugar
$^1/_4$ teaspoon salt
$1^1/_4$ cups milk
1 egg
2 teaspoons vanilla
1 teaspoon almond extract
3 tablespoons butter, melted
$^1/_2$ cup sliced almonds, toasted
maple syrup for garnish

Preheat the waffle iron.

Combine flour, ground almonds, baking powder, sugar, and salt in large bowl.

In another bowl, whisk together milk, egg, vanilla, almond extract, and butter. Pour into flour mixture and stir to combine.

Pour onto the waffle maker and follow the manufacturer's instructions. Sprinkle with toasted almonds and serve with maple syrup.

MAKES 4

LEMON POPPY SEED WAFFLES

This delicious combination should wake up sleepy taste buds in a flash.

1 cup all-purpose flour
1 teaspoon baking powder
1/4 teaspoon baking soda
1/4 teaspoon salt
2 tablespoons poppy seeds
2 tablespoons sugar
3/4 cup buttermilk
1/2 stick butter, melted
1 egg
grated zest of 1 lemon
juice of 1 lemon
maple syrup or "Raspberry Sauce"
   (see page 89) for garnish

Preheat the waffle iron.

Combine flour, baking powder and soda, salt, poppy seeds, and sugar in large mixing bowl.

In another bowl, whisk together buttermilk, butter, egg, lemon zest and juice. Pour into flour mixture and stir just to combine.

Pour onto the waffle maker and follow the manufacturer's instructions. Serve with "Raspberry Sauce" or maple syrup.

MAKES 4

PECAN WAFFLES

*For those in search of an intense pecan experience—
sturdy brown waffles to swoon over.*

$1^1/_2$ cups pecan halves
$^3/_4$ cup all-purpose flour
1 teaspoon baking soda
1 teaspoon baking powder
$^1/_2$ teaspoon salt
2 tablespoons brown sugar
$^1/_4$ teaspoon cinnamon
$^1/_8$ teaspoon ground ginger
1 cup buttermilk
2 eggs
2 tablespoons butter, melted
maple syrup for garnish

Preheat the waffle iron. Spread nuts on a baking sheet and toast in a 350 degrees F oven about 10 minutes. Cool and finely chop ½ cup nuts.

Combine flour, baking soda and powder, salt, brown sugar, cinnamon, and ginger in large mixing bowl.

In another bowl, whisk together buttermilk and eggs. Pour into dry ingredients. Gently whisk to combine. Stir in butter and chopped nuts.

Pour onto the waffle maker and follow the manufacturer's instructions. Scatter remaining toasted pecans over top and serve with maple syrup.

MAKES 4

SOUR CREAM COFFEE CAKE WAFFLES

These substantial waffles are rich and yellow from extra eggs. They serve as a nice platform for a scoop of vanilla ice cream.

1 cup all-purpose flour
1 teaspoon baking soda
1 teaspoon baking powder
1/2 teaspoon salt
3 tablespoons sugar
1 cup sour cream
1 tablespoon vanilla
3 eggs
4 tablespoons butter, melted
maple syrup for garnish
1/2 cup toasted pecan halves and cinnamon
    sugar for garnish (optional)

Preheat the waffle iron.

Combine flour, baking soda and powder, salt, and sugar in large bowl.

In another bowl, whisk together sour cream, vanilla, and eggs. Pour into flour mixture and stir to combine. Stir in butter.

Pour onto the waffle maker and follow the manufacturer's instructions. Sprinkle the waffles with pecans and cinnamon sugar, if desired, and serve with maple syrup.

Makes 4

FRESH GINGER BUTTERMILK WAFFLES

3/4 cup all-purpose flour
1 teaspoon baking powder
1/2 teaspoon baking soda
2 tablespoons sugar
1/2 teaspoon salt
1 cup buttermilk
3 eggs, separated
3 tablespoons butter, melted
1 tablespoon freshly grated ginger
2 teaspoons grated lemon zest
maple syrup for garnish

Preheat the waffle iron.

Combine flour, baking powder and soda, sugar, and salt in a large bowl.

In another bowl, whisk together buttermilk, egg yolks, butter, ginger, and lemon zest. Pour into flour mixture and stir to combine.

In a third bowl, beat egg whites until stiff. Gently fold into batter.

Pour onto the waffle maker and follow the manufacturer's instructions. Serve with maple syrup.

MAKES 4

PEANUT BUTTER WAFFLES

Waffles for breakfast, waffles for lunch, waffles for supper. With peanut butter waffles in the freezer, every meal is a snap.

1 cup all-purpose flour
1 tablespoon baking powder
$\frac{1}{2}$ teaspoon cinnamon
2 eggs
$\frac{1}{3}$ cup crunchy peanut butter
$\frac{1}{4}$ cup brown sugar
2 tablespoons peanut or vegetable oil
1 cup milk
confectioners' sugar for dusting
jelly *or* maple syrup for garnish

Preheat the waffle iron.

In a large bowl, mix together flour, baking powder, and cinnamon.

Combine the eggs, peanut butter, sugar, oil, and milk in blender. Process to blend. Pour into flour mixture and stir to combine.

Pour onto the waffle maker and follow the manufacturer's instructions. Sprinkle these dark brown waffles with confectioners' sugar and serve with your favorite jelly for dipping, or top with maple syrup.

MAKES 4 OR 5

DESSERT CAKES

HUNGARIAN CREPES

To build a Hungarian-style pancake cake known as a palacsinta *with these fine crepes, stack a dozen or so with a thin mortar of jam and nuts between the layers, and a coating of thin chocolate sauce on the top. Cut in wedges and serve as you would cake.*

3 eggs
1 cup milk
1/3 cup club soda, freshly opened
1 teaspoon vanilla
1 cup cake flour *or* 3/4 cup plus 2 tablespoons
    all-purpose flour
3 tablespoons sugar
1/4 teaspoon salt
butter for frying
apricot jam, finely chopped walnuts, and
    confectioners' sugar

Combine the eggs, milk, soda, and vanilla in blender. Pulse to blend. Add flour, sugar, and salt and blend about 30 seconds to thoroughly combine. Pour into a bowl and let sit at room temperature about 1 hour to thicken to consistency of cream.

To cook, heat an 8-inch crepe or frying pan over medium-high heat. Melt a tablespoon or two of butter in the pan and pour it into a small bowl, leaving a fine film in the pan. (Add a few drops more of melted butter as needed between additions.) Pour a scant ¼ cup of batter into the pan and swirl to evenly coat. When edges are set and golden, in a minute or two, turn with a spatula and cook the second side until golden. Stack crepes with waxed paper between each. (The stack can be packed in a zipper-lock bag and frozen.)

To serve singly, spread each with a teaspoonful of jam and sprinkle lightly with nuts. Roll, cigarette-style, and sprinkle with sugar.

MAKES 10, SERVES 5

COCOA CAKES

For the chocoholic in your group, here is a dark chocolate crepe to serve as a sponge for chocolate sundae toppings.

> 1 cup milk
> 2 tablespoons unsweetened Dutch cocoa
> $1/4$ cup sugar
> $1/2$ teaspoon vanilla
> 2 eggs
> $3/4$ cup all-purpose flour
> 2 tablespoons butter, melted
> butter for frying
> chocolate ice cream and hot fudge sauce for garnish

Combine the milk, cocoa, and sugar in a small saucepan. Cook over medium heat, stirring frequently, until cocoa and sugar dissolve and the milk nearly comes to a boil. Let cool.

Combine vanilla, eggs, and flour in blender. Pulse to blend. Pour in cooled milk and butter mixture. Blend until smooth and pour into a bowl. (Batter does not have to sit to thicken.)

To cook, heat an 8-inch crepe or frying pan over medium-high heat. Melt a tablespoon or two of butter in the pan and pour it into a small bowl, leaving a fine film in the pan. Pour in a scant $\frac{1}{4}$ cup of batter and swirl to evenly coat. When edges are set, in a minute or two, turn with a spatula and cook the second side until golden. (Add a few drops of melted butter as needed between additions.) Stack crepes with waxed paper between each. Serve topped with chocolate ice cream and hot fudge sauce.

Makes 8, serves 4

PUFFED PANCAKE WITH APPLES AND CINNAMON

The apple topping and batter can be prepared hours before guests arrive. Just reheat topping and pop the pancake in the oven when dinner is finished for an impressive dessert.

> 5 tablespoons butter
> 3 apples, peeled, cored, and sliced (Fuji or Gala are best)
> 1/4 cup maple syrup
> 1 tablespoon plus 2 teaspoons lemon juice
> 1/4 teaspoon cinnamon
> 2 eggs
> 1/2 cup all-purpose flour
> 1/2 cup milk
> 1/2 teaspoon vanilla

Melt 2 tablespoons of the butter in a large skillet over medium-high heat. Sauté apples until golden, about 8 minutes. Add maple syrup, lemon juice, and cinnamon and reduce heat to low. Cook, stirring occasionally, until tender but not mushy, 15 to 20 minutes. Set aside.

Whisk together eggs, flour, milk, and vanilla in a bowl.

Preheat oven to 400 degrees F.

In another ovenproof 10-inch skillet, melt the remaining butter over medium-high heat. Pour in the batter, swirl to evenly coat, and place in oven. Bake about 15 minutes until golden and puffed—the peak in the center will deflate. Transfer to serving platter with spatula, top with sautéed apples, and cut into wedges to serve.

MAKES 1, SERVES 4

EASY TOPPINGS

APRICOT SAUCE

1 (17-ounce) can apricot halves in syrup
1½ tablespoons Kirsch or Amaretto

Drain the fruit, reserving the syrup.

Combine the fruit, ½ cup of the syrup, and Kirsch or Amaretto in blender or food processor. Purée until smooth and pour into a small saucepan. Cook over low heat just to warm. Transfer to a pitcher to serve.

MAKES 1 CUP

COCONUT SYRUP

Coconut is a natural with banana pancakes or any nut pancake or waffle.

1 (14.5-ounce) can unsweetened coconut milk
1 cup sweetened shredded coconut
1/2 cup brown sugar

Combine all of the ingredients in a heavy saucepan. Bring to a boil, reduce to a simmer, and cook 20 minutes. Transfer to blender and purée until smooth. Serve warm.

MAKES 2 CUPS

RASPBERRY SAUCE

Raspberries are a natural complement to lemon, sour cream, cottage cheese, and, of course, chocolate.

1 pint fresh raspberries
   or 1 (10-ounce) package frozen raspberries
$^1/_3$ cup sugar

Combine raspberries and sugar in small saucepan and cook over low heat, stirring occasionally, about 5 minutes, until berries dissolve. Strain to remove seeds, if desired. Serve hot.

MANGO SAUCE

1 1/3 cups chunked mango, fresh or frozen and
    thawed
1/4 cup lemon juice
2 tablespoons sugar
1/4 teaspoon cinnamon

Combine all of the ingredients in a blender
and purée. Transfer to small pan and heat
through.

MAKES 1 1/2 CUPS

MOCHA SAUCE

This sauce is made to order for "Cappuccino Cakes"
(see page 28) or "Cocoa Cakes" (see page 82).

$^1\!/_2$ cup heavy cream
$^1\!/_4$ cup brown sugar
2 tablespoons coarsely ground espresso beans
1 tablespoon chocolate syrup
$^1\!/_2$ cup plain yogurt

Combine the cream, sugar, and coffee in a small heavy saucepan. Cook over low heat, stirring occasionally, until sugar is dissolved and coffee infused, about 3 minutes. Watch carefully, to avoid boiling over.

Pour through a fine strainer into a bowl. Stir in chocolate syrup. Add yogurt and stir to combine. Do not reheat.

MAKES 1 CUP

PEAR BUTTER

Fruit butters are a delicious substitute for butter and syrup.

2½ pounds ripe pears, peeled, cored, and
    roughly chopped
½ cup sweet dessert wine
2 tablespoons lemon juice
½ cup sugar
½ teaspoon cinnamon

Combine pears, wine, and lemon juice in heavy saucepan. Bring to boil, reduce to simmer, cover, and cook until pears are soft, about 20 minutes.

Transfer to a food processor or blender and purée. Pour back into pot and add sugar and cinnamon. Cook over low heat until thickened to taste, 1 to 2 hours. Cool and store in glass jars in the refrigerator.

MAKES ABOUT 2 CUPS

ORANGE MAPLE SYRUP

Serve with "Sour Rye Cakes" (see page 34), "Orange Chocolate Chip Waffles" (see page 60), or just plain buttermilk pancakes.

1/2 cup maple syrup
2 tablespoons orange juice
2 tablespoons butter
1 (11-ounce) can mandarin orange segments, drained

In a small saucepan, combine all ingrediants. Cook over low heat until butter is melted and sauce is warm.

MAKES 1 1/2 CUPS

PINEAPPLE RUM SAUCE

This sauce lends a tropical touch to plain, but sub-
stantial hotcakes such as wheat or buckwheat.

1 (8-ounce) can crushed pineapple in syrup
2 tablespoons maple syrup
1 tablespoon rum

In a small saucepan, combine all the ingredients. Cook over low heat until heated through.

MAKES 1 CUP

CONVERSIONS

LIQUID
1 Tbsp = 15 ml
1/2 cup = 4 fl oz = 125 ml
1 cup = 8 fl oz = 250 ml

DRY
1/4 cup = 4 Tbsp = 2 oz = 60 g
1 cup = 1/2 pound = 8 oz = 250 g

FLOUR
1/2 cup = 60 g
1 cup = 4 oz = 125 g

TEMPERATURE
400° F = 200° C = gas mark 6
375° F = 190° C = gas mark 5
350° F = 175° C = gas mark 4

MISCELLANEOUS
2 Tbsp butter = 1 oz = 30 g
1 inch = 2.5 cm
all-purpose flour = plain flour
baking soda = bicarbonate of soda
brown sugar = demerara sugar
confectioners' sugar = icing sugar
heavy cream = double cream
molasses = black treacle
raisins = sultanas
rolled oats = oat flakes
semisweet chocolate = plain chocolate
sugar = caster sugar